JUST AS ARTISTS FEEL AN
INSATIABLE DESIRE TO PAINT
AND POETS HAVE TO GIVE FREE
REIN TO THEIR THOUGHTS,
I WAS DRIVEN BY AN
UNCONTROLLABLE URGE
TO SEE THE WORLD.

IDA PFEIFFER

·I·D·A·

AND THE WORLD BEYOND MOUNT KAISERZIPF

The life of Ida Pfeiffer, globe-trotter,
narrated and illustrated by Linda Schwalbe

North
South

1. IDA

I WAS NOT
SHY BUT AS
WILD AS A BOY,
AND BRAVER AND
BOLDER THAN
MY BROTHER.

Vienna 1802

When I was five years old,
my head was full of adventures.

I gazed up at the mountains and wondered what everything looked like behind Mount Kaiserzipf.

There were sure to be amazing things just waiting to be discovered. One day I would be a research scientist and go into the jungle and study unknown species of butterflies.

That was what I dreamed of.

I went on various adventurous expeditions with my brothers.

We often played outside.
I studied and collected insects.

My mother was not too keen on all this.
She thought adventures were not the right
and proper thing for girls.

I should stay at home and become a perfect young lady.

In the meantime, my brothers left home and went out into the world.

Time passed, and I became nice and respectable.
I got married and had children.
My mother was delighted.

Later, my grown-up
children went their
own ways.

It seemed to me that
all of a sudden I had become
quite old and gray.

Then something
that I had long since
forgotten came back
into my head.
My dream of travel
and adventure.

Why should I sit all day long at the window dreaming about such things?
There was still so much of the world to explore!
But what exactly does an adventurer need to pack in her suitcase?

2. THE JOURNEY

EVERY NEW MOVE
REVEALED BEAUTY.
I DIDN'T KNOW
WHICH WAY TO TURN
MY EVER-EAGER EYES.

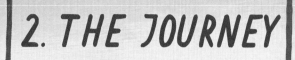

I sailed all over the world.
Sometimes dolphins would accompany our ship
on the way during our long voyage across the ocean.

I lived like all the other sailors, and ate pea soup and salted meat.

Sometimes there were strong winds,
and then we landlubbers got seasick.

At night I had to tie myself to the bunk with my clothes and coat in order not to fall out.

The storm gave us
a good shaking.
Suddenly someone
shouted:

"Land ahead!"

3. THE ISLAND

I WAS SEIZED
BY A STRANGE FEELING
WHEN FOR THE FIRST TIME
IN MY LIFE I SET FOOT
IN A DIFFERENT PART
OF THE WORLD.

IT WAS AS IF I HAD
ONLY NOW SEPARATED
FROM MY HOME,
WHICH FELT LIKE
A MILLION MILES AWAY.

It was also the first time in months that my feet were standing on firm ground.

There was a world completely
unknown to me, waiting to be explored.

It seemed to me that this place was full of mysteries.
Maybe I would find some rare species of butterflies here.

The jungle became denser and darker.
Suddenly something moved in the undergrowth.

There were other people apart from us on the island.
And so we met Ayu and her friends.

I explained that we were here to do some research. Ayu invited us to follow her, and she took us to a place that I only knew from the books I had read.

We came to a hidden valley beside a lake.
So this was Ayu's home.

We were given a warm welcome and celebrated all through the night.

As a farewell we promised
never to forget each other.

When I write about my adventures today, I think of Ayu.
And I wonder if she has discovered that unknown species of butterfly
that I was looking for.

Ida Pfeiffer was the first woman to travel around the world alone and without financial support. She was one of the most famous travel writers of the nineteenth century.

Ida was born in Vienna, Austria, in 1797, and was the third child of Alois and Anna Reyer. The family ran a prosperous business, and the seven children were given a strict, military-style upbringing, but it was also egalitarian. Ida was nine years old when her father died. From then on, while Ida could only dream of traveling and exploring, her mother did everything in her power to guide her along more conventional paths.

Eventually Ida married Anton Pfeiffer, a lawyer; but the marriage was not a happy one, and the couple lived separately. Ida raised her two sons alone in Vienna, but her financial situation was always precarious.

Not until she was forty-four and her two sons had grown up did Ida dare to follow her dreams of becoming an explorer. Her first journey was to Palestine and Egypt. A publisher persuaded her to publish her record of that journey; the book was successful, and the royalties financed her subsequent expeditions.

Ida Pfeiffer's main interests were natural history—she collected many specimens from the plant and animal kingdoms—and photography, and she spoke several languages.

She set out on her first round-the-world trip in 1846, and it took her two years. Subsequently her account, *A Woman's Journey Round the World*, was published in three volumes, and this finally established her popularity and recognition as an important travel writer. The book was translated into many languages. Her second journey

around the world (1851–1855) included the islands of Indonesia, where she lived for a while among the indigenous tribes.

Back in Vienna, Ida Pfeiffer would have liked to settle down to a quieter life, but one year later she went to Madagascar and Mauritius. She became involved in the political unrest there, was arrested in Madagascar, and later expelled. She was now physically very weak and returned to Vienna, but not long afterward died from the aftereffects of malaria.

Ida Pfeiffer was a fascinating character who defied social convention to make her own way into the unknown. She explored uncharted territories, driven by an insatiable curiosity about the world and a desire for adventure.

Linda Schwalbe studied illustration at the Burg Giebichenstein University of Art and Design Halle and at the Berlin University of the Arts. Inspired by discoveries and adventures, music and nature, she is happiest painting with acrylics. *Ida and the World Beyond the Kaiserzipf* is Linda Schwalbe's first picture book. She lives and works in Leipzig.

First published in the United States, Great Britain, Canada, Australia, and New Zealand in 2020
by NorthSouth Books Inc., an imprint of NordSüd Verlag AG, CH-8050 Zürich, Switzerland.

Distributed in the United States by NorthSouth Books Inc., New York 10016.
Library of Congress Cataloging-in-Publication Data is available.
Printed at Livonia Print, Riga, Latvia 2019
ISBN: 978-0-7358-4420-9
1 3 5 7 9 • 10 8 6 4 2
www.northsouth.com

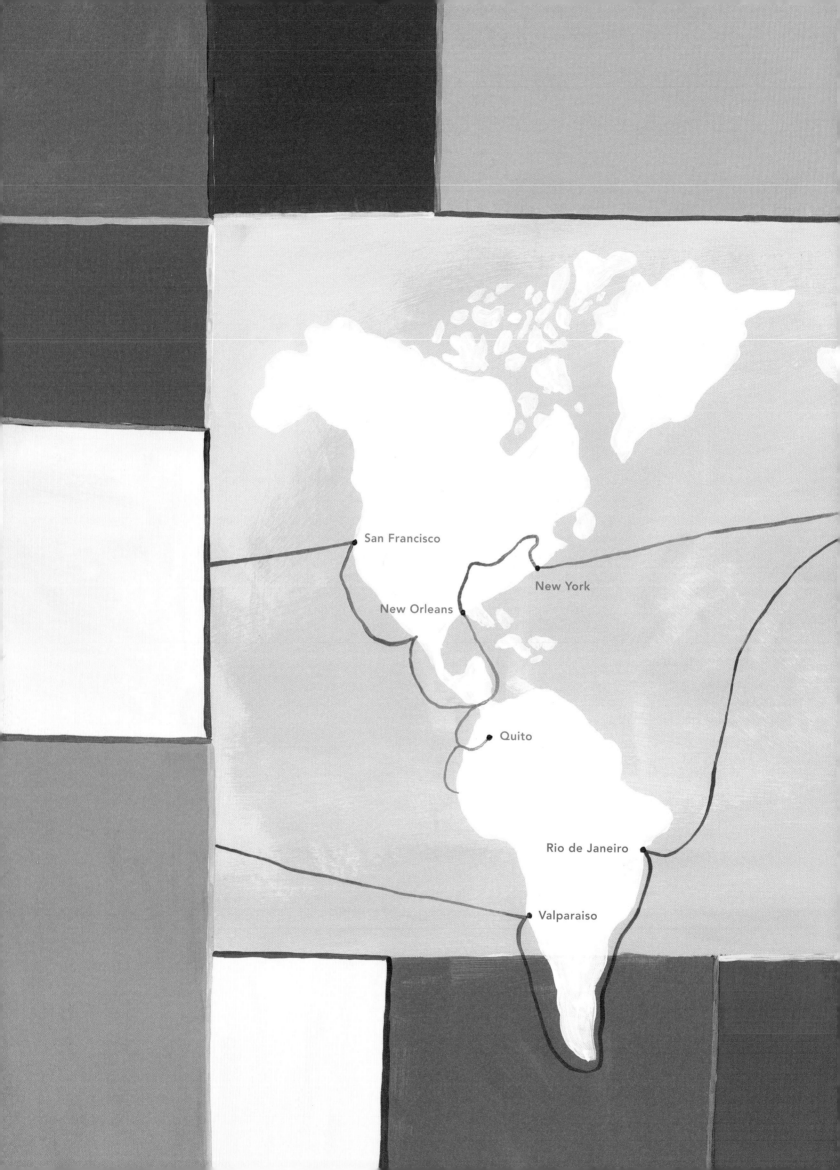